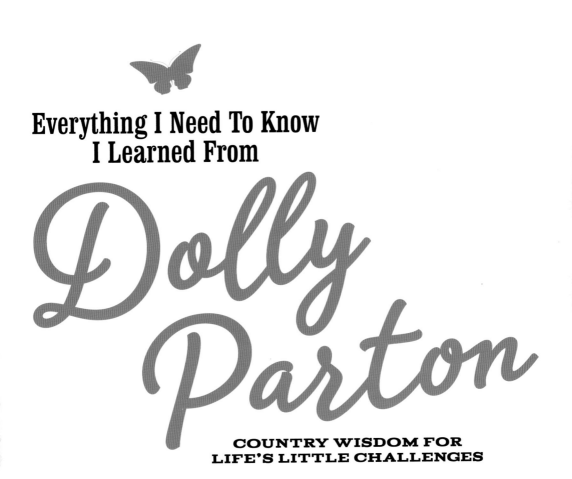

Everything I Need To Know I Learned From Dolly Parton

COUNTRY WISDOM FOR LIFE'S LITTLE CHALLENGES

All Hail the Queen of Country

ONLY ONE NAME in music brings people together from all walks of life: Dolly Parton. Her literal rags-to-riches story of an Appalachian girl leaving her Tennessee mountain holler to take on Nashville and beyond is just as much a testament to her musical talents as her drive to stay true to what she values most: freedom, faith, family and love. From opening her own theme park to creating an international children's literacy program to branching into Netflix territory and more, it's clear that even after more than 60 years in the spotlight, Dolly's just getting started. In the pages that follow, you'll find dozens of life lessons inspired by some of her greatest hits, favorite movie moments, real-life anecdotes as well as several quotes that stand as darn good advice on their own. No matter where you come from, Dolly's got a word of backwoods wisdom that will warm your heart and set you on a course to your dreams.

Dolly Parton at her theme park, Dollywood, in Pigeon Forge, Tennessee, c. 1993. Dollywood first opened its doors in 1986.

Dolly Parton is all smiles with Barbara Walters in 1977.

Own Who You Are

"I'm very real where it counts, and that's inside."

—DOLLY PARTON

AS DOLLY BEGAN to make a name for herself as a country-singing sensation on the national stage, in 1977, she sat down for an unforgettable interview with Emmy Award-winning journalist Barbara Walters. After discussing the singer's humble upbringing, the conversation shifted to Dolly's undeniably bold image—her curvaceous figure and eye-catching sense of style. "You don't have to look like this," Walters said. "You're very beautiful, you don't have to wear the blonde wigs, you don't have to wear the extreme clothes, right?"

Own Who You Are

Dressed to the nines in her powder blue satin best, her larger-than-life platinum curls coiffed perfectly in place, Dolly said, "It's certainly a choice. I don't like to be like everybody else. I've often made the statement that I would never stoop so low as to be fashionable, that's the easiest thing in the world to do."

Walters continued, "But do you ever feel like you're a joke, that people make fun of you?"

"Oh I know they make fun of me," Dolly admitted. "But actually, all these years the people have thought the joke was on me, but it's actually been on the public...I am sure of myself as a person. I am sure of my talent. I'm sure of my love for life and that sort of thing. I am very content, I like the kind of person that I am. So, I can afford to piddle around and do-diddle around with makeup and clothes and stuff because I am secure with myself."

Take it from Dolly: There's no need to apologize for knowing exactly who you are.

A portrait of Dolly at the Holiday Inn in Chicago, Illinois, April 30, 1977.

Dolly Parton shares the stage with Johnny Cash at the Country Music Association Awards in Nashville, Tennessee, in 1978. "I Will Always Love You" won Dolly Female Vocalist of the Year at the 1975 CMA Awards.

Trust Your Instincts

"Find out who you are and do it on purpose."

—DOLLY PARTON

AFTER JOHNNY CASH told the 13-year-old Dolly Parton to follow her instincts and continue pursuing a career in music, she took that advice to heart. But years later, when Elvis Presley wanted to cover one of her songs, Dolly had to choose whether she should give up half of her rights to the song to have it covered by the King. While everyone around her said she was crazy to not take the deal, Dolly stuck to her guns, saying, "Something in my heart says, 'Don't do that.'" The song? "I Will Always Love You," which Whitney Houston later covered for *The Bodyguard* (1992). That soundtrack became one of the best-selling movie soundtrack albums of all time. Don't sell yourself short. Trust your gut—it could really pay off in the long run.

Dolly Parton performs in Carthage, Tennessee, on October 13, 1973.

Fight for What's Yours

"You could have your choice of men
But I could never love again
He's the only one for me
Jolene"

—DOLLY PARTON, "JOLENE"

ORE THAN FOUR decades after its 1973 release, Dolly's second No. 1 hit song, "Jolene," continues to cast its forlorn spell on just about everyone. Using only 200 words, Dolly paints the portrait of a desperate woman at her most vulnerable, forced to confront the unnerving reality that her beloved has caught the eye of a beautiful woman on the prowl. Overcome with dread and unhinged by the very real prospect

Dolly arrives at Heathrow Airport to take part in the eighth International Festival of Country Music in London, England, on April 16, 1976.

Fight for What's Yours

of losing her lover for good, the frightened, nameless narrator summons her courage and tracks down the red-haired, green-eyed Jezebel in her midst. But rather than cut her down outright, or worse—concede defeat and watch her make off with her man—the singer takes a surprising third route, walking a razor-thin line that alternates between awe-struck admiration and dire warning. Laying all her cards on the table, she pleads with heartbreaking earnestness, "Please don't take him just because you can," while nonetheless staking her claim: "He's the only one for me."

Having based the song on a real-life experience in which her husband briefly took notice of a flirtatious red-headed teller at their bank, Dolly lightheartedly recalled, "She had everything I didn't, like legs—you know. She was about six feet tall and had all that stuff that some little short, sawed-off honky like me don't have." With its universal themes of vulnerability, inadequacy and jealousy, "Jolene" is arguably the most relatable song in Dolly's robust repertoire, and has been covered by artists across multiple genres. The lesson: Everyone feels insecure sometimes. But the things you love are worth fighting for every way you can.

Dolly Parton as Miss Mona Stangley in *The Best Little Whorehouse in Texas* (1982).

"Well, I always just thought
if you see somebody without
a smile, give 'em yours!"

～～

MISS MONA STANGLEY,
*THE BEST LITTLE WHOREHOUSE
IN TEXAS* (1982)

Dolly Parton
in 1951.

You Can Be Rich in Spirit

"My coat of many colors
That my momma made for me
Made only from rags
But I wore it so proudly"

—DOLLY PARTON, "COAT OF MANY COLORS"

LONG BEFORE HER days as a rhinestone-studded superstar, Dolly grew up dirt poor, one of 12 children living in a cramped backwoods mountain cabin with no electricity and no indoor plumbing. With barely any money to scrape together, Dolly's mother made her daughter a coat out of various scraps of fabric she was able to scrounge so the young

You Can Be Rich in Spirit

girl would have something warm to wear in the coming autumn, telling her the Bible story about Joseph and his "coat of many colors" as she sewed. While such a simple, patchwork garment might inspire embarrassment in some, for Dolly it was a symbol of her mother's love. Even though classmates teased her for wearing it at school, the future songwriter refused to let cruel words make her feel anything less than special. Dolly commemorates this memory in the song "Coat of Many Colors" as an ode to her family. Out of the more than 3,000 songs she's written, she cites this one as her favorite—a personal reminder that her truly remarkable, literal rags-to-riches story was made possible through the values espoused by her parents. As the song later goes, "One is only poor, only if they choose to be." No matter what opportunities and comforts come your way, nothing makes you richer than the love of your family.

Dolly Parton attends the Hollywood premiere of her made-for-television film *Dolly Parton's Coat of Many Colors* on December 2, 2015.

Find Your Passion

"I love that I've been able to make a living at something I love to do."

—DOLLY PARTON

EVEN IF YOU haven't written more than 3,000 songs like Dolly has, if you're serious about honing your chosen craft, you're bound to get into a creative streak every now and then. You might even be lucky enough to have an especially productive session like the one Dolly did back in the early 1970s, when she claimed to have written "Jolene" and "I Will Always Love You" in the same day. And while it's true the likes of Whitney Houston may not be called upon to belt out your latest, greatest ballad, it's a timely reminder that each and every day, we are all given the same 24-hour window of opportunity to make the most of our passions in life, so long as we keep up the hard work.

Dolly Parton
c. 1970.

Half of Life is Just Showing Up

Taking that first step toward any goal can feel daunting. But you'll never know what dreams might fall into place until you put yourself out there and make a move.

AFTER SINGING LIVE on Knoxville radio stations at the tender age of 10, by 1959, Dolly Parton was ready to take her talent to the next level. With support from her uncle, musician Bill Owens, Dolly made the rounds playing regional country music circuits, winning hearts and making friends along the way—including Carl and Pearl Butler, a husband-and-wife country duo who did more than show up when Dolly and Bill arrived one night at the Grand Ole Opry.

Dolly Parton (back row, right) celebrates Christmas with her family in 1960.

A crowded night at the Grand Ole Opry in Nashville, Tennessee, in 1946.

Half of Life is Just Showing Up

Knowing their ambitious young friend was keen on becoming a star, the Butlers persuaded the chart-topping Cajun artist Jimmy C. Newman to give up one of his prized Saturday night slots so that Dolly could sing her heart out. Impressed with her gumption, Newman graciously allowed Dolly to take his place. And when the 13-year-old took the stage to make her Opry debut, she was introduced by none other than her biggest crush: the Man in Black himself, Johnny Cash.

"We've got a little girl here from up in East Tennessee," he began. "Her daddy's listening to the radio at home and she's gonna be in real trouble if she doesn't sing tonight, so let's bring her out here."

"As I heard the band play my introduction," she later recalled, "I lifted my head and looked up toward the lights. I smiled at the people in the balcony and then let 'er rip." She belted out George Jones's song, "You Gotta Be My Baby," and impressed the crowd so much they demanded an astonishing three encores, a dazzling start to a stellar career. It just goes to show you never know what doors might open when you dare to knock.

14-year-old Dolly
in 1960.

Never Stop Chasing Your Dreams

*"Above everything else I've done,
I've always said I've had more guts than I've got talent."*

—DOLLY PARTON

GRADUATING HIGH SCHOOL is a praiseworthy milestone for any student, and at her graduation ceremony, 18-year-old Dolly knew exactly where she was headed next. As she recounts in her 2012 book *Dream More: Celebrate the Dreamer in You*, when all the graduates were asked in turn to share a few words about the lives they hoped to live, Dolly proudly announced, "I'm going to Nashville and I'm gonna be a star." But rather than applaud her ambition, "the whole place laughed out loud." Little did the naysayers know Dolly had already packed her bags. Less than 24 hours later, she hopped aboard a bus bound for Music City and never looked back. When you choose to chase your dreams, you never know just how far you'll go.

"I'm not offended by all of the dumb blonde jokes because I know I'm not dumb... and I also know that I'm not blonde."

DOLLY PARTON

Dolly Parton
in 1981.

Don't Underestimate Anyone

"Just because I'm blonde
Don't think I'm dumb
'Cause this dumb blonde ain't nobody's fool"

—DOLLY PARTON, "DUMB BLONDE"

O N FEBRUARY 13, 1967, 21-year-old Dolly Parton released her first full-length solo album, *Hello, I'm Dolly*, on Monument Records. Never one to beat around the bush, she starts things off with a bang with the song "Dumb Blonde." From the moment the needle hits the vinyl, Dolly's all fired up about setting the record straight, laying down the law in no uncertain terms about who she is and what she's all about.

Dolly Parton's mile-high hair in 1965.

Porter Wagoner (seated) and Dolly Parton with Speck Rhodes (far left) and Porter's backup band, "The Wagonmasters," in 1968.

Don't Underestimate Anyone

Nursing a broken heart after enduring a fallout with her lover, she sings, "You called me a dumb blonde." It's a charge she doesn't deny—the over-the-top blonde part, anyway, as evidenced by her beehive on the album cover. "Ah, but somehow I lived through it," she continues. "And you know if there's one thing this blonde has learned / Blondes have more fun." Dolly knows she may look like a joke, but the joke's on anyone who underestimates her. It's a clever crafting of the image that will soon become her signature look, a call to remember the brain beneath the larger-than-life blonde wig.

The snappy Smoky Mountain Songbird in the making soon caught the attention of country star Porter Wagoner, who invited her to join his variety television show following the departure of his previous female singing partner. Although fans of "Pretty Miss Norma Jean" took a little while to warm to Dolly, the show would eventually help put the 21-year-old singer on the trail to stardom. A rebuke to all those who would seek to belittle her lighthearted spirit with a hurtful stereotype, "Dumb Blonde" reminds us to never judge a book by its cover—especially one in five-inch heels.

True Love Lasts

"Like everyone else, we have our ups and downs, but we have always been and will always be committed to our love for each other."

—DOLLY PARTON

ON HER FIRST day in Nashville, Tennessee, an 18-year-old Dolly was strolling outside a laundromat when a handsome young man called out to her from his pickup truck. His name was Carl Dean, and after striking up a friendly conversation, it was clear the two were immediately taken with each other. Two years later, Dolly and Carl tied the knot. And after more than five decades of wedded bliss, it's clear the country superstar and her low-key husband accept each other for who they are—he stays out of the spotlight, while she tours to her heart's content, even when that means spending months apart. The two lovebirds are living proof that a deep, abiding respect for one another is the glue that holds a family together.

Dolly Parton
c. 1966.

Dolly Parton poses for an interview in 1998. The country singer's signature blonde wig collection numbers in the hundreds.

Make Your Own Luck

"These old bones will tell your story
These old bones will never lie
These old bones will tell you surely
What you can't see with your eye"

—DOLLY PARTON, "THESE OLD BONES"

SOME OF US develop the uncanny ability to clearly see our future, whether that means having the vision and drive to manifest our dreams or being clairvoyant in the spiritual sense. It's an intriguing concept Dolly explores in one of her more recent beloved numbers, the 2002 track "These Old Bones." The narrator describes a kindly, witchy mountain woman whose assorted collection of bones, when scattered, can foretell

Dolly Parton performs at Irving Plaza in New York City on July 10, 2002.

Dolly with Kathleen Turner on the set of Dolly Parton's *Heartstrings* for the "These Old Bones" episode.

events to come. Just before this fabled "Old Bones" passes away, the narrator seeks her out for their one and only meeting, only to learn that she, too, has the gift of prophecy.

"That was a lady that had kind of predicted in my young years … she said I was anointed, and I was going to do great things," Dolly later recalled, "and I asked Mama, 'What's that word mean?' She said, 'That just means God had his hand on you.' And so, I feel like he did."

As the song concludes, the singer shares her own inspiring insight: Perhaps it wasn't the bones themselves that spelled out the path that lay before her but the loving hand that threw them again and again in hopes of helping others find their way. "You just remember that the magic is inside you," she says, matter-of-factly. "There ain't no crystal ball."

Dolly knows there's nothing that can warm your heart and change your life like the transforming power that comes with believing in yourself.

"You'll never do a whole lot unless you're brave enough to try."

DOLLY PARTON

Dolly Parton
c. 1965.

Know Your Worth

"Yes, I've made my mistakes
But listen and understand
My mistakes are no worse than yours
Just because I'm a woman"

—DOLLY PARTON, "JUST BECAUSE I'M A WOMAN"

EMERGING FROM HER Smoky Mountain holler as an ambitious up-and-coming country music talent could not have been easy for Dolly Parton. Exposed to abject poverty in her youth, she soon had to contend with the sexism of the music industry that pressured her to delay marrying the love of her life, Carl Dean, lest the move strike the wrong chord with fans. But Dolly has always dared to be different, and her 1968 sophomore

Know Your Worth

album, *Just Because I'm a Woman*, shows the not-so-dumb blonde was just getting started.

"I'm sorry that I'm not the woman you thought I'd be," she tells her frustrated lover in the title track. It seems her love life has been more colorful than he imagined, knowledge he now holds against her. She makes it clear she's "no angel;" instead, she's the sadder-but-wiser product of a "man that let me down." Rather than rehash the stories of her past, the singer takes a moment to call out the hypocrisy of the gender paradox at hand: that men are told to sow their oats while women are expected to remain chaste. "Just think of all the shame / You might have brought somebody else," she warns him, pointing to his own past discretions.

It takes a brave person to call out unsavory truths. Be your own advocate, and know that your worth is not defined by anyone's expectations but your own.

Dolly onstage
c. 1977.

Learn to Laugh at Yourself

*"I know some of the best Dolly Parton jokes.
I made 'em up myself."*

—DOLLY PARTON

HAVING MODELED HER appearance on the town tramp from her youth, Dolly Parton's got no shortage of reasons to laugh at herself. In a 2012 interview on *Nightline*, she explained, "I had never seen anybody, you know, with the yellow hair all piled up and the red lipstick and the rouge and the high heeled shoes, and I thought, 'This is what I want to look like.'" Later in life when Dolly's signature style inspired a local look-alike contest, the superstar decided to crash the event for kicks, exaggerating her hair and makeup for added effect. When she took the stage, however, not only did no one recognize her—"I got the least applause." Like Dolly knows, keep your heart humble and you'll always find a reason to laugh.

Dolly Parton smiles with Dolly impersonator Jason CoZmo at the Los Angeles premiere of the Netflix film *Dumplin'* (2018) on December 6, 2018.

Dolly Parton, Lily Tomlin and Jane Fonda in a scene from *9 to 5* (1980). The popular comedy marked Dolly's acting debut.

Suffer No Fools

When others speak ill of you, feel free to go straight to the source and set the record straight. You might even make a few friends.

*D*OLLY GAINED a whole new legion of fans by making her transition to the silver screen in the 1980 workplace revenge comedy *9 to 5*. Dolly plays Doralee Rhodes, a spirited secretary who is overworked, underpaid and weary of her bigoted boss, Franklin Hart, Jr. (Dabney Coleman), whose incessant sexist remarks and obnoxious come-ons have worked on her last nerve. To her disgust, Doralee discovers he's been spreading rumors about the two having an affair that never happened. Outraged at being

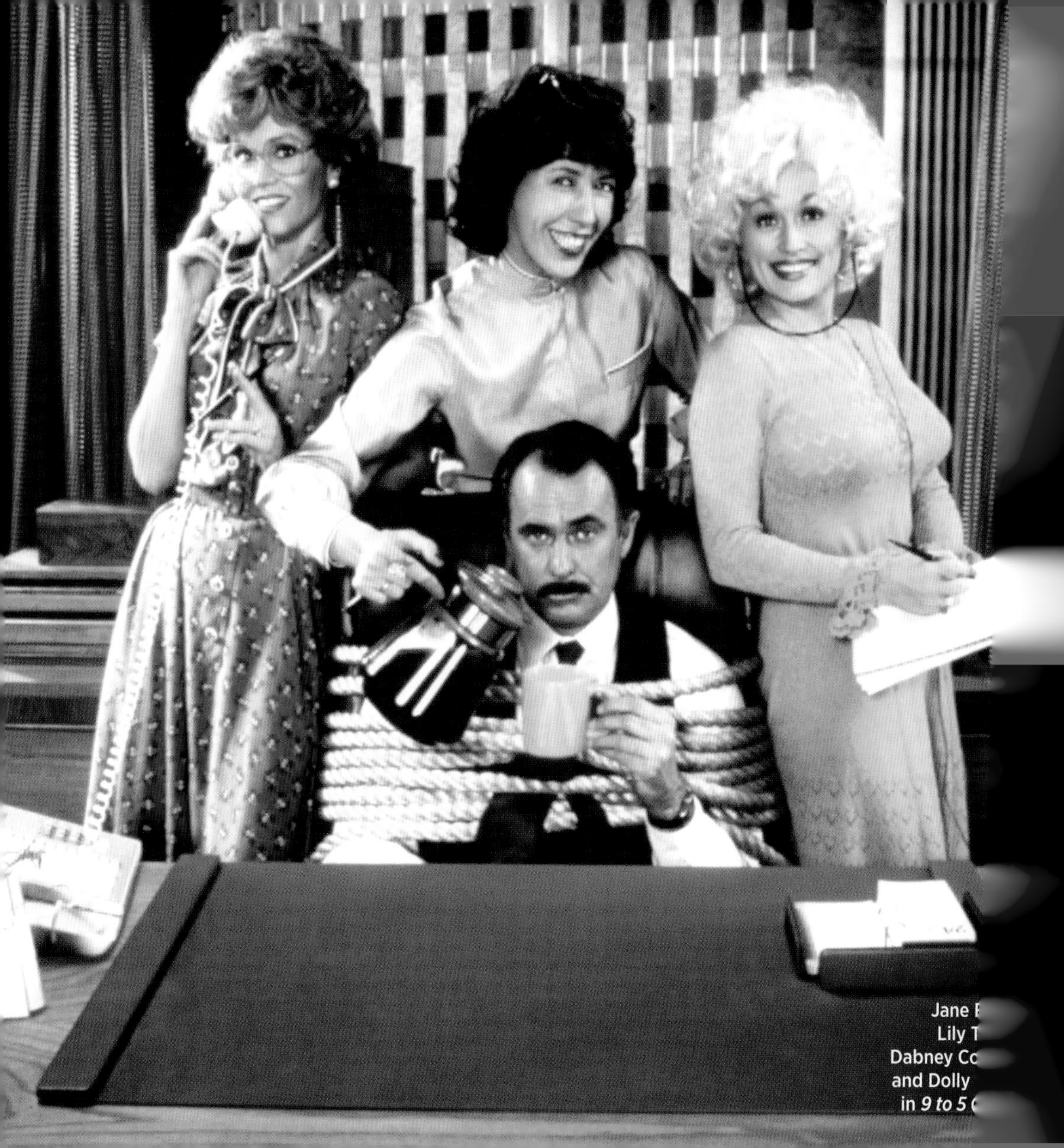

Jane F
Lily T
Dabney Co
and Dolly
in *9 to 5* (

Suffer No Fools

characterized as a "dime-store floozy," Doralee joins forces with two of her equally exploited colleagues—Judy Bernly (Jane Fonda) and Violet Newstead (Lily Tomlin)—to give their boss a lesson he'll never forget. Her first order of business: confronting Hart head-on. After hearing Violet refer to her as their boss's "mistress," Doralee immediately takes Hart to task, saying, "Look, I've got a gun out there in my purse. And up to now, I've been forgiving and forgetting because of the way I was brought up. But I'll tell you one thing: If you ever say another word about me or make another indecent proposal, I'm gonna get that gun of mine and I'm gonna change you from a rooster to a hen with one shot!"

Doralee makes it clear she won't tolerate being slandered or mistreated, least of all by her boss. And if someone isn't treating you with the respect you deserve, feel free to let them know that actions have consequences.

Be Your Own Hero

*"At last I have caught up with you and you're a sight to see
Could this really be my outlaw lover J.J. Sneed
Could a woman with a painted face and pretty sweet disguise
Turn your heart against me with her evil cunning eyes"*

—DOLLY PARTON, "J.J. SNEED"

T'S A SAD truth that not everyone we care about is willing to go the distance for us the same way that we do for them. We often learn this hard lesson when a friend or loved one lets us down in our hour of need. In the case of Dolly's song "J.J. Sneed," that lack of support comes with a heaping side of betrayal, prompting the singer to take matters into her own hands.

Dolly Parton
c. 1972.

Dolly Parton in the
"J.J. Sneed" episode
of *Dolly Parton's
Heartstrings* (2019).

Be Your Own Hero

Released as part of her 1971 album *Joshua*, "J.J. Sneed" tells the story of an outlaw and his lover on the run. The daring couple lead an exciting life robbing banks, taking names and staying one step ahead of the authorities. When J.J. is gunned down during one botched getaway, rather than write him off as a lost cause and make off with the money herself, the singer tends to his wounds and nurses him back to health. But there's no honor in this thief, and J.J. pays back his devoted companion's kindness by taking up with another woman.

Having suffered the ultimate disrespect, the scorned narrator tracks J.J. down. Gun in hand, she appoints herself his judge, jury and executioner, telling him plainly, "I hope you feel no pain." It's a level of betrayal she cannot abide, even if that means saying goodbye to her partner in crime. When the chips are down, don't expect anyone to have your back. At the end of the day, the only person you can count on is yourself.

"I was the first woman to burn my bra—it took the fire department four days to put it out."

DOLLY PARTON

Dolly Parton attends the California premiere of *Steel Magnolias* in Century City, California, November 9, 1989.

Dolly Parton
takes the stage
at the Los Angeles
Convention Center on
February 8, 2019.

Have a Little Faith

"We all need to have hope that there's something bigger than we are."

—DOLLY PARTON

SINCE SHE WAS knee-high to a grasshopper, one aspect of Dolly's life has eclipsed even her musical talents: her faith. As the granddaughter of a Pentecostal preacher, 6-year-old Dolly sang hymns and played guitar during worship services at church, developing her performing abilities early in life. The rhinestone-studded songstress has long credited her enduring success to divine providence—the guiding hand that sustained her family through years of severe poverty and steered her toward an incredible destiny. According to Dolly, "We grew up believing that through God all things are possible. I think I believed that so much that I made it happen." Stay true to your beliefs, especially when the going gets tough. You'll find your way.

Always Be Kind

"The best friend that I ever had was Cracker Jack
But he was more than that
A playmate, a companion
He was love and understanding"

—DOLLY PARTON, "CRACKER JACK"

WHEN IT COMES to unconditional love, dogs in particular can teach us a great deal about how to give generously of ourselves without expecting anything in return. And when you help an animal in need, you make a new friend for life, a lesson Dolly learned as a child that she explores in the 1974 song "Cracker Jack."

Drawing on the memories of her sister's real-life playful pup, Dolly spins a tale that harkens back to one of the sunniest times of her hard-pressed childhood. After stumbling upon a lonesome

Dolly Parton,
c. 1974.

Loretta Lynn greets Dolly Parton backstage at the 53rd annual CMA Awards in Nashville, Tennessee, on November 13, 2019.

Always Be Kind

stray wandering along a riverbank, she nurses the starving dog back to health and the two become inseparable. "Cracker Jack would run to meet me / After school each day," she sings, "He'd jump and wag his tail / And look at me as if to say / 'I love you and I've missed you / And I'm glad you're home again.'" The new best friends spend their days getting into mischief and enjoying each other's company in the great outdoors, running through the woods to their heart's content. But as all of us who have been lucky enough to have pets know, these good times don't last forever; eventually our beloved companions pass on. "He only lives in memories now," she sings, and we feel her loss.

The kind of love shown by animals like Cracker Jack is a precious gift, one that stays with us forever and encourages us to show kindness whenever we can. You could change a life, and you might even make a lifelong friend.

Five-year-old Dolly in 1951.

What Doesn't Kill You Makes You Stronger

"Storms make trees take deeper roots."

—DOLLY PARTON

I N 1955, as Avie Lee Parton prepared to deliver her ninth child, she told a 9-year-old Dolly that this infant would be hers to take care of. But the Partons' unbridled joy soon turned to heartbreak when newborn baby Larry breathed his last breath just hours after his birth. Reeling with grief and devastated at having lost the brother promised to her special care, Dolly and her family rallied together in their mourning, wrapping their wounded hearts with the unbreakable bond of familial love. And like a rainbow following a storm, nearly two years later, the Partons welcomed their newest sibling, Floyd, who grew up to become one of Dolly's songwriting companions. Not everything happens for a reason. In times of tragedy and hardship, lean on your loved ones to see your way through.

Stand by the People You Love

"I can't live without you if the love was gone
Everything is nothing if you got no one"

—KENNY ROGERS & DOLLY PARTON, "ISLANDS IN THE STREAM"

EVEN THOUGH DOLLY Parton has penned plenty of hits over the course of her career, "Islands in the Stream" has the unique honor of being the only hit in her extensive collection that was written by the Bee Gees. It's also the song that brought her together with fellow country legend Kenny Rogers, who decided to make it his own after the track's intended singer, Marvin Gaye, turned it down.

In fact, "Islands in the Stream" was supposed to be a solo. But over the course of his recording sessions, Kenny and his team found

Dolly Parton with Barry Gibb of the Bee Gees in 1983.

Dolly and Kenny Rogers reunite for a duet in 1989.

Stand by the People You Love

themselves struggling to create the ideal sound that would take the song to the next level. When Dolly happened to be in the same studio that day, Kenny tracked her down and asked if she wouldn't mind giving the song a whirl as a duet. She agreed, and the rest is chart-topping music history. Rogers later recalled, "Once she came in [the studio], that song was never the same. She lit it up and we became good friends from that point on."

"Islands in the Stream" centers on a pair of lovers taking a moment to bask in the warmth of their steadfast respect and affection for one another. "Tender love is blind," they sing, "It requires a dedication /All this love we feel needs no conversation." Built on trust, the sweethearts know it's a love that can last forever so long as they both stay the course. As the song goes, "We start and end as one."

True to their 1983 hit, Dolly and Kenny's friendship lasted decades, right until Kenny's passing in 2020. When you find someone who understands where you're coming from and what you're all about, never let them go. Whether romantic or platonic, those relationships make life worth living.

"*It's hard to be a diamond in a rhinestone world.*"

―――――⬥―――――

DOLLY PARTON,
"TENNESSEE HOMESICK BLUES"

Dolly Parton wows the crowd at the Day on the Green Concert in Oakland, California, on May 28, 1978.

Dolly Parton as Shirlee Kenyon in *Straight Talk* (1992).

You Don't Always Need a Plan

**Things won't always go the way we envision.
But that doesn't mean we can't make the most of our skills
along the way. After all, all we can do is our best.**

*I*N *STRAIGHT TALK* (1992), Dolly plays Shirlee Kenyon, a small-town dance instructor from Arkansas who gets booted from her studio for dishing more life advice than dance techniques. Fresh out of a job, Shirlee hopes to turn over a new leaf by moving to Chicago where, after a few dead ends, she soon lands a new gig manning the switchboard at a local radio station. But when the fresh-faced newcomer gets mistaken for a

You Don't Always Need a Plan

newly-hired call-in therapist, she finds herself put on the spot and forced to go live on the air.

As longtime listeners share their burdens, however, the former dance teacher lets her instincts take the lead and begins dispensing sage advice to caller after caller. While "Doctor Shirlee" gains a legion of rabid new followers eager to hear her down-home wisdom, Shirlee struggles with the dishonesty of her much-loved moniker when she's off the air. When pretending to be a real doctor weighs too heavily on her conscience, she comes clean on the air and promptly quits the radio station. But much to her delight, Shirlee's devoted fanbase demands her return to broadcasting, which she happily accepts, sans "Doctor."

Even though she hadn't signed up for it, Shirlee stumbled upon an opportunity and leaned on her talents, as well as her character, to see her way through. It's a reminder that even when the path forward isn't what we imagined, we can still remain open to new possibilities as long as we stay true to ourselves.

Dolly Parton
in a scene from
Straight Talk (1992).

Dolly sings as
Jake Farris in
Rhinestone (1984).

Find the Silver Lining

"The way I see it, if you want the rainbow, you gotta put up with the rain."

—DOLLY PARTON

FIVE YEARS before she charmed audiences in *Steel Magnolias*, Dolly starred alongside Sylvester Stallone in the 1984 film *Rhinestone*. Dolly plays Jake Farris, a country singer who finds herself tasked with turning an arrogant New York cab driver named Nick (Stallone) into a bona fide country music star. A financial failure, the film was pulled from theaters after just a month, and while Stallone has publicly regretted appearing in *Rhinestone*, Dolly never has. In fact, she credits the soundtrack with some of her best work, including the two hit singles, "Tennessee Homesick Blues" and "God Won't Get You." Rather than walk away from acting, Dolly kept her chin up and chose to look at the good that came from her efforts, even when they weren't smash successes.

Dolly Parton and Bonnie Raitt perform at the "Women Rock! Songs from the Movies" concert in Hollywood, California, on October 1, 2003.

Seize the Moment

"I think I'll dry these useless tears and get myself together
I think I'll wander down the hall and have a look around
'Cause I can't stay inside this lonely room and cry forever
I think I'd really rather join 'em two doors down"

—DOLLY PARTON, "TWO DOORS DOWN"

L IFE IS FILLED to the brim with exciting opportunities for those who know where to look. But it's equally important to remember that the party won't always find you—sometimes you need to put your best foot forward and track it down yourself. This was something Dolly learned in 1977, when the touring singer found herself holed up in her hotel room one evening. Feeling down and lonesome, she heard the lively sounds of

Dolly Parton gets close with Mick Jagger at the Bottom Line nightclub in New York City on May 14, 1977.

Dolly smiles backstage at the Day on the Green concert in Oakland, California, on May 28, 1978.

Seize the Moment

a party taking place just steps from her door. Her band had taken advantage of the downtime to cut loose and let the good times roll by throwing an impromptu get-together. Dolly had a choice: wallow in her loneliness and hope someone would eventually come find her, or shake off the blues by joining in the fun.

For as much as we like to be remembered when it comes to social gatherings, there will be moments when it's on us to make the first move. Never one to turn down a good time, Dolly made up her mind to pick herself up and head on down. The 1978 country pop hit "Two Doors Down" fills in the rest.

"I can't believe I'm standing here dry-eyed, all smiles and talkin'," she sings, "making conversation with the new love I've found." And well before the song fades into its brassy, joyous outro, it's clear things have worked out in her narrator's favor far beyond what she could've imagined, all because she simply showed up. Like the old country saying goes: Make hay while the sun shines. You never know what you might find.

Never Stop Growing

"Adjusting to the passage of time, I think, is a key to success and to life: just being able to roll with the punches."

—DOLLY PARTON

WITH MORE THAN six decades of performing music under her belt, no one would blame the Queen of Country Music if she ever decided to hang up her hat and rest on her hard-earned laurels. But in a 2020 interview with *60 Minutes Australia*, Dolly said, "I don't plan to retire. I just turned 74 and I plan on being on the cover of *Playboy* magazine, again." In fact, the tireless icon has branched out in recent years to captivate a whole new generation of fans by writing the music and lyrics to *9 to 5: The Musical*, penning original new songs for the 2018 Netflix film *Dumplin'*, producing the 2019 Netflix series *Dolly Parton's Heartstrings* and more, proving legends of her caliber always strive for growth.

Dolly Parton greets fans at the Broadway premiere of *9 to 5: The Musical* on April 14, 2009.

"If you don't like
the road you're walking,
start paving another one."

DOLLY PARTON

Know When to Go Your Own Way

"If I should stay
I would only be in your way
And so I'll go, but I know
I'll think of you each step of the way"

—DOLLY PARTON, "I WILL ALWAYS LOVE YOU"

AFTER RELEASING HER spirited debut album, 1967's *Hello, I'm Dolly*, Dolly Parton received the offer of a lifetime. Porter Wagoner, a massive country star and esteemed member of the Grand Ole Opry known for his trademark pompadour and flashy rhinestone cowboy style, invited Dolly to join him on his popular musical variety show, *The Porter Wagoner Show*. The beaming young

Dolly and Porter Wagoner singing a duet on *The Porter Wagoner Show*, c. 1972.

Dolly Parton and Porter Wagoner in 1973.

Know When to Go Your Own Way

blonde quickly proved a ready-for-primetime tour de force, and the singing duo's powerful onscreen chemistry took the music program to the top of the charts, making it the No. 1 syndicated country show of the 1960s and 70s.

But after seven glorious years of performing downhome duets before starry-eyed audiences, Dolly correctly sensed it was high time to take her act solo. After all, she'd received no shortage of glowing reviews for putting out hits like 1971's "Joshua" and the haunting 1973 ballad "Jolene." Breaking the news to Porter, however, would require a bold gesture, so the country singer opted to set her conflicted feelings to music. Putting pen to paper, Dolly drew on her abiding gratitude to flesh out one of the greatest love songs of all time as a thank you to her longtime mentor. The next day, she sang "I Will Always Love You" for Porter in his office. Her heartfelt lyrics not only moved him to tears, but helped him understand her intentions in a way that words alone could not.

It takes courage to step out into the world on your terms, so be sure to start off on the right foot by thanking the ones who helped you on your journey.

Lily Tomlin,
Dolly Parton
and Jane Fonda
in *9 to 5* (1980).

Commit to Your Plans

"Yeah, I think we can pull it off. I really do."

—DORALEE RHODES, *9 TO 5* (1980)

IN *9 TO 5* (1980), Dolly's character, Doralee Rhodes, teams up with her equally fed-up colleagues, Judy Bernly and Violet Newstead, to kidnap their boss, Franklin Hart Jr., and run the department while he's indisposed. Risking jail time, the three hold him hostage in his own house while enacting policies that raise morale and improve the lives of their fellow employees with resounding success. But when Hart regains his freedom and threatens to expose their deeds, rather than bail on each other to seek their own immunity, the women stick together and emerge victorious when the chairman of the board transfers Hart to Brazil. The takeaway from this story? When you see a plan through to the end, you can achieve virtually anything you set your mind to.

Dolly Parton shines in the spotlight, c. 1976. As of 2019, the singer has received two stars on the Hollywood Walk of Fame.

The Heart Wants What It Wants

*"Here you come again
Just when I've begun to get myself together
You waltz right in the door
Just like you've done before
And wrap my heart 'round your little finger"*

—DOLLY PARTON, "HERE YOU COME AGAIN"

TEN YEARS AFTER her debut album made waves on the country music scene, Dolly was ready to take her sound to the next level. As fate would have it, the talented songwriting duo Barry Mann and Cynthia Weil had just penned a pop number written with Brenda Lee in mind. But when Lee turned it down, Dolly got to pick it right up and make it her own.

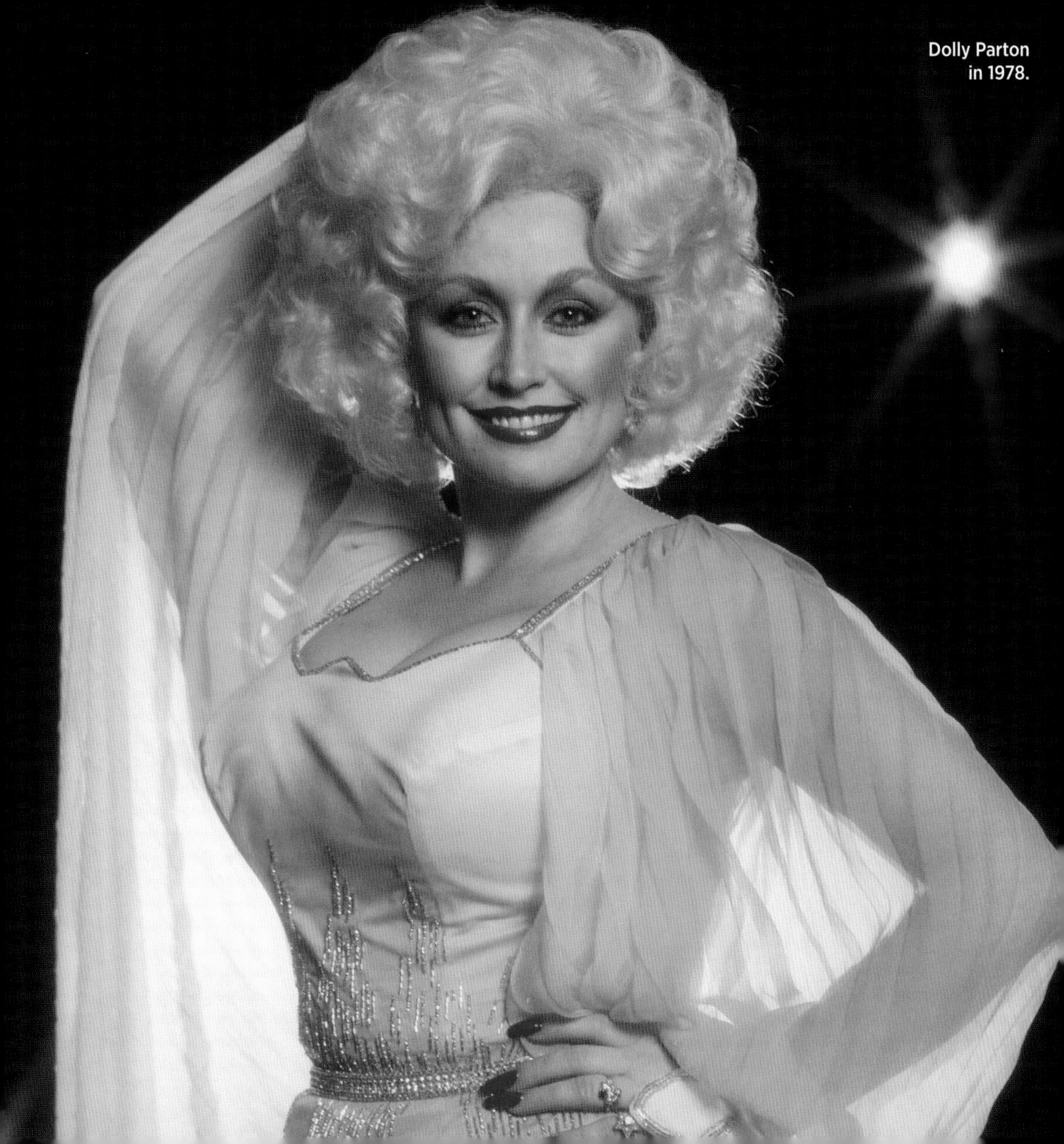

Dolly Parton
in 1978.

The Heart Wants What It Wants

Knowing the crossover to pop might give her diehard country fans whiplash, she added a steel guitar into the mix to round things out with a familiar twang. The result? 1977's "Here You Come Again," which topped the charts for a whopping five weeks and earned her a Grammy Award for Best Female Country Vocal Performance.

This unprecedented career move did not come without complaint, however. When her loudest detractors accused her of abandoning the music that put her on the map, Dolly cooly replied, "I'm not leaving country. I'm taking it with me."

"When I made my change to do what I'm doin' now to appeal to a broader audience, people said, 'You can't do that, because you are going to wreck your whole career. . . . You just better think about that, girl,'" she told *Playboy* in 1978. But she didn't back down, and that same year, the singer took home the County Music Association's Entertainer of the Year Award.

Others might not share your vision for success, and that's OK. Don't let that stop you from making your dreams a reality.

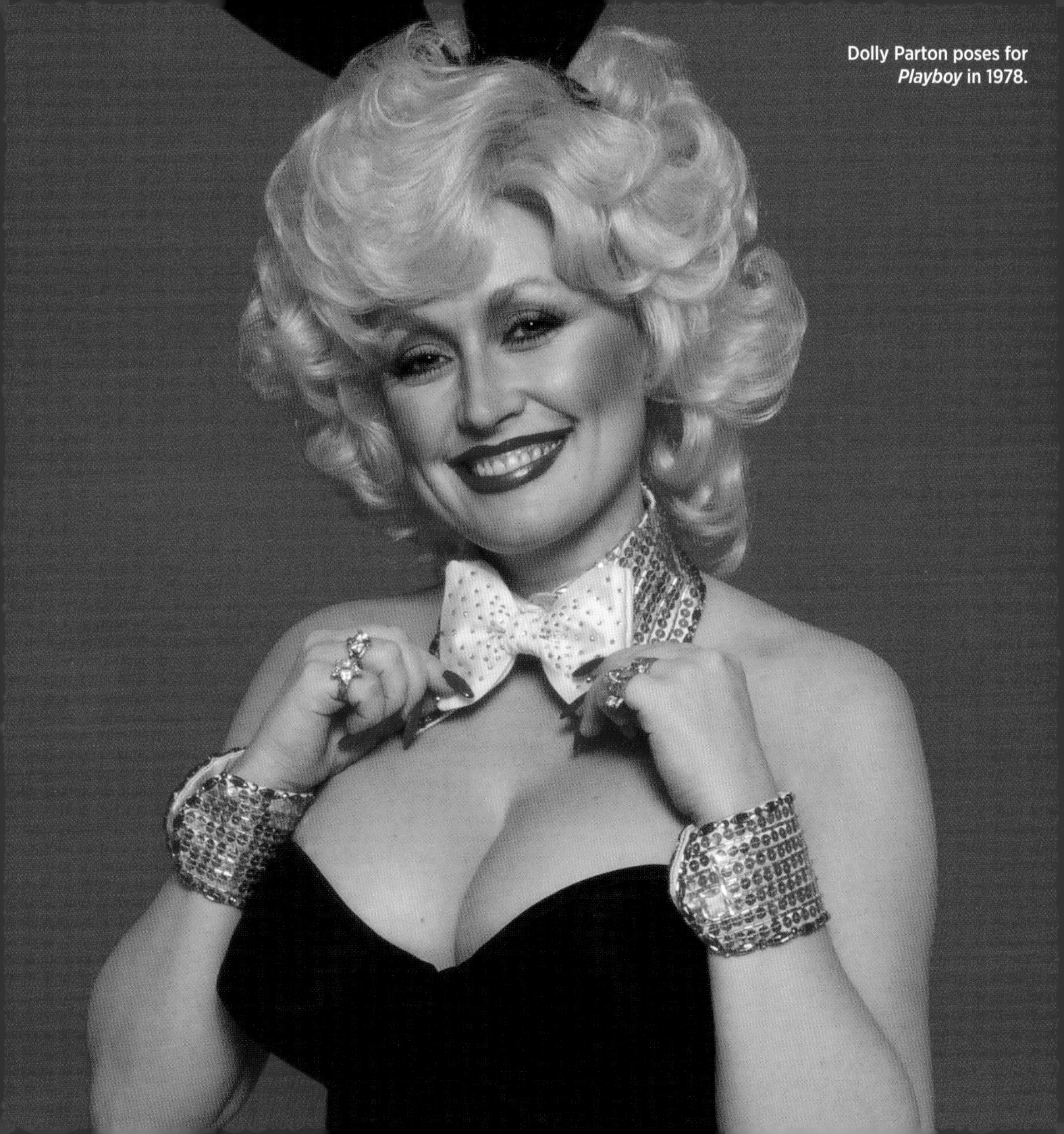

Dolly Parton poses for *Playboy* in 1978.

Dolly Parton as
Truvy Jones in *Steel
Magnolias* (1989).

A Little Empathy Goes a Long Way

"I have a strict policy that nobody cries alone in my presence."

—TRUVY JONES, *STEEL MAGNOLIAS* (1989)

ONE SCENE IN the feel-good Southern classic *Steel Magnolias* (1989) perfectly captures Dolly's capacity for kindness. As hairdresser Truvy Jones, Dolly lends a helping hand when a good friend's daughter, Shelby Eatenton-Latcherie (Julia Roberts), visits the salon to have nearly all of her gorgeous locks chopped off. As a busy first-time mother, Shelby believes it will "make things as simple as possible" when caring for her little one. But when she lays eyes on Truvy's handiwork, she tears up, shocked and saddened at the sight of her new look. Sensing her young friend is struggling to accept herself, Truvy tells her, "Oh, sweetheart, don't. Please don't cry or I will too." Like all sympathetic friends, she gently reminds us that we don't have to carry our burdens alone.

"*I am that saying:
'The higher the hair,
the closer to God.'*"

DOLLY PARTON

Dolly Parton in
Rhinestone (1984).

There's No Place Like Home

"The greenest state in the land of the free
And the home of the Grand Ole Opry
Is calling me back to my Smoky Mountain home"

—DOLLY PARTON, "TENNESSEE HOMESICK BLUES"

A MULTIGENERATIONAL STAR LIKE Dolly Parton can choose to make her home wherever she pleases, especially when she's no stranger to touring. But even when success brings you to every corner of the globe, for Dolly, home has always been the mountains of Tennessee, and "Tennessee Homesick Blues" shines a light on all the happy memories that fondly call her back time and again.

There's No Place Like Home

Written for the 1984 film *Rhinestone*, the song plays up a handful of the pure and simple joys so endearing to country living, like fishing, hunting and enjoying a hearty slice of "Mama's homemade chocolate cake." And even though Dolly wrote these lyrics with her character, Jake Farris, in mind, any listener can tell these cheerful recollections come straight from the heart.

By the time she filmed *Rhinestone*, Dolly had cemented her place not only as a successful crossover star, moving into prime pop territory with 1977's "Here You Come Again," but a bona fide actress, sharing the silver screen with the likes of Jane Fonda and Lily Tomlin in *9 to 5* (1980). To top it all off, she even had her own New York City apartment on Fifth Avenue overlooking Central Park. But despite all the glitz and glamour of her new digs, Dolly knew that no amount of Empire City elegance could outshine the humble, wholesome places of her youth. No matter where your talents might take you, nothing soothes the soul and fills the spirit like all the cherished fixin's that put the "sweet" in home sweet home.

Dolly Parton and Sylvester Stallone saddle up in *Rhinestone* (1984).

Dolly Parton and Lee Majors in a scene from *A Smoky Mountain Christmas* (1986).

Real Beauty Comes from the Heart

"But when you get right down to it, it's not the package that really matters. It's what's inside the wrapping. It's what's down deep in your heart."

—LORNA DAVIS, *A SMOKY MOUNTAIN CHRISTMAS* (1986)

IN DOLLY PARTON'S holiday classic, 1986's *A Smoky Mountain Christmas*, Dolly plays Lorna Davis, a kindhearted country singer who wakes up one morning to find seven orphans hiding out in her holiday cabin. Rather than send them back to their orphanage, she graciously decides to care for the children herself, instilling them with valuable life lessons about love and family. When one young girl, Cindy, confides her hope that a new dress will make her feel pretty, Lorna sees the moment as a teachable one. Clothes might give us confidence, she says, but the source of true beauty can only be found in the goodness of our hearts.

Kenny Rogers and Dolly Parton perform in Los Angeles, California, in 1990. The two sang their final duet together at Rogers's farewell tribute concert in 2017.

Dolly performs at the Mill Run Theater in Niles, Illinois, August 29, 1977.

Judge People for Who They Are

"Folks said he was a mean and a vicious man
And you better not set foot on his land
But I didn't think nobody could be that mean"

—DOLLY PARTON, "JOSHUA"

RUMORS HAVE A way of spreading like wildfire, and can be just as damaging socially. When you know the havoc hearsay can wreak on good people firsthand, ignore the haters and go straight to the source. That's what Dolly did, and it made for a lesson she'll never forget.

As the title track of Dolly's seventh studio album, "Joshua" refers to a real-life recluse Dolly knew growing up in the Smoky

Judge People for Who They Are

Mountains of East Tennessee. Despite his penchant for living alone, the kindly hermit nevertheless enjoyed entertaining visitors by strumming his banjo. Dolly draws on these memories to flesh out her own unique fictional tale of a young woman who hears about "a mean and vicious man" living in a shack on the outskirts of town. When her curiosity gets the better of her, she heads on down to meet this nameless person face-to-face "and just find out if all them things I'd heard was true." She soon encounters "the biggest man I'd ever seen," and despite his gruff welcome, the two come to find they've got a lot in common—namely, they're both alone in the world. It's this shared common ground that leads the singer and her new acquaintance, Joshua, to become friends. By the end of the song, the two have fallen in love, content to have found in each other someone to call their own.

Don't get caught up in gossip. Keep an open mind and let people show you who they are. It might even make for a great story.

Dolly Parton arrives at Heathrow Airport in London, England, in 1977.

Dolly Parton
meets with fans
at Peaches Records,
May 3, 1977.

"When someone shows me
their true colors,
I believe them."

DOLLY PARTON

Walk a Mile in Someone Else's Shoes

"I know this dress I'm wearing doesn't
hide the secret I've tried concealing
When he left he promised me he'd be back
by the time it was revealing"

—DOLLY PARTON, "DOWN FROM DOVER"

EVERY LIFE IS filled with twists and turns. Despite our best intentions, things don't always turn out the way we hope. Sometimes we're left to pick up the pieces alone. Dolly has never shied away from writing songs about tough topics. From "The Bridge" to "My Blue Ridge Mountain Boy" to "Evening Shade,"

Dolly Parton
in 1976.

Walk a Mile in Someone Else's Shoes

it's clear the country singer knows a thing or two about broken dreams and the difficult choices desperate people make when pushed to their breaking point. "Down from Dover," from her 1970 album *The Fairest of Them All*, falls squarely into this category. Told from the perspective of an unmarried pregnant woman waiting for her long-lost lover to return, it's a heartbreaking story about unkept promises and a hopeful outcast left to fend for herself.

When the singer's parents discover the true nature of their daughter's growing waistline, rather than treat her with kindness, they call her a fool and kick her out of the house. With no family or friends willing to support her, she nonetheless manages to find a kindly old woman who doesn't ask questions and agrees to take her in. But this moment of solace doesn't last. "Something's wrong," she sings when the baby finally arrives. She takes its stillness as a sign that her lover will never return.

The fact is, you never know what someone else might be going through. Be the person who chooses to show compassion rather than judgement. There's a chance you're the only one who will.

Dolly Parton and Burt Reynolds in *The Best Little Whorehouse in Texas* (1982).

You Are Worthy of Love

Regardless of your background, your reputation does not define whether or not you deserve kindness and affection. You already do, right now.

*I*N THE CLASSIC musical comedy *The Best Little Whorehouse in Texas* (1982), Dolly plays Miss Mona Stangley, the sassy madam of the Chicken Ranch and a hooker with a heart of gold. Despite the scandalous nature of her line of work, Mona maintains a longstanding romance with Sheriff Ed Earl Dodd (Burt Reynolds), who sees to it that the brothel be allowed to continue its business with little outside interference.

You Are Worthy of Love

But when an out-of-town television personality (Dom DeLuise) airs a live exposé of the illegal activities taking place at the Chicken Ranch—as well as Ed Earl's role in the arrangement—the small town haunt finds itself thrown into the national spotlight. With tensions running high, the frustrated lawman loses his temper—he bitterly calls his lover a "whore," and the two part ways. The wave of negative publicity prompts the Governor (Charles Durning) to order the beloved bordello shuttered indefinitely, leaving Mona to pack her things and begin looking for work elsewhere. But as Mona prepares to leave the storied establishment for the last time, much to her surprise, the still-smitten sheriff arrives to confess his love and ask for her hand in marriage.

Not everyone will approve of how you choose to live your life. But the ones who matter most will see the best in you no matter what.

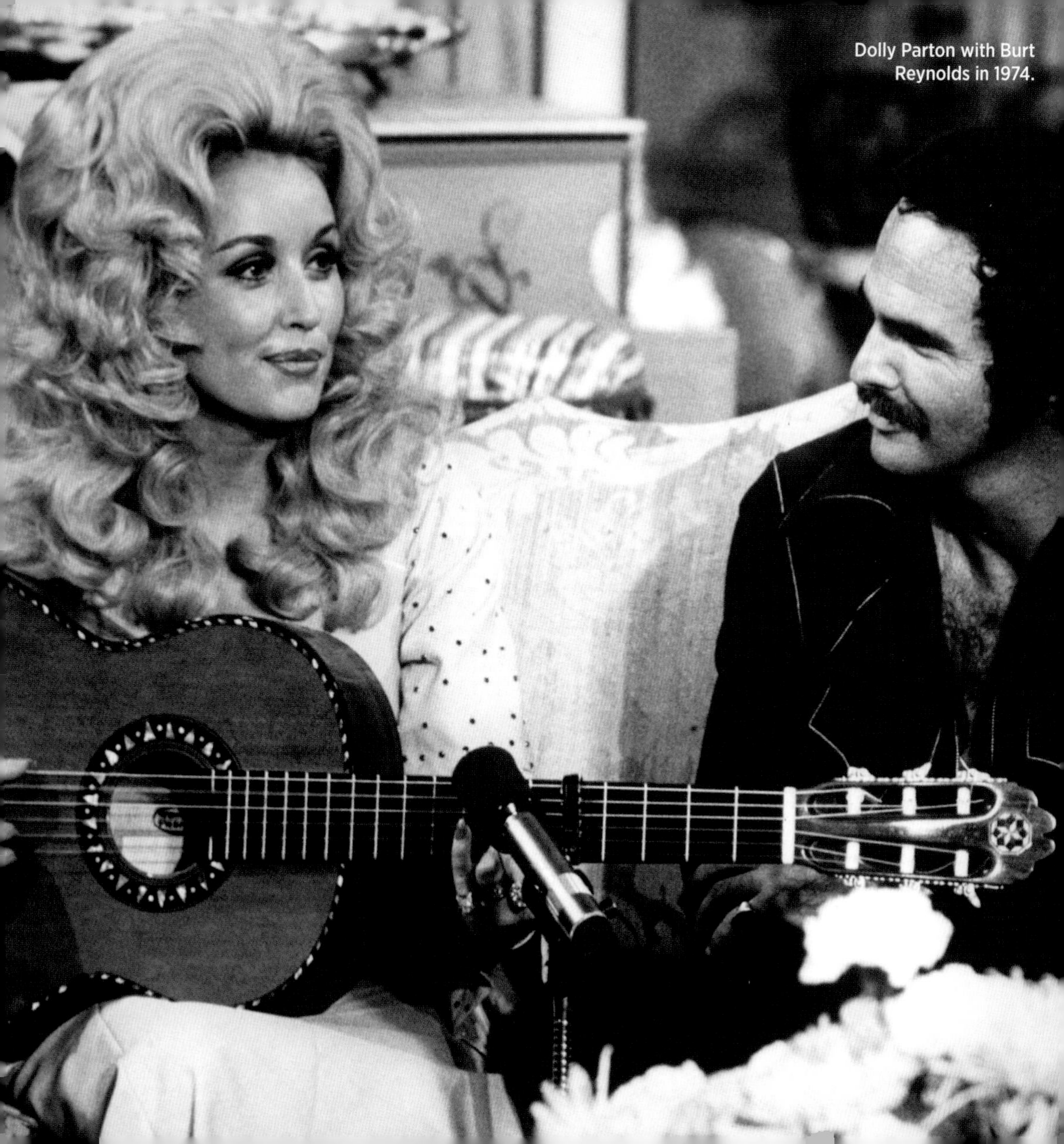

Dolly Parton with Burt
Reynolds in 1974.

Dolly's all smiles in an undated photo with the Mandrell Sisters. Dolly has five sisters of her own: Willadeene, Stella, Cassie, Frieda and Rachel.

Dolly Parton greets young fans at the launch of her Imagination Library in Rotherham, England on December 5, 2007.

Be a Leader

"If your actions create a legacy that inspires others to dream more, learn more, do more and become more, then you are an excellent leader."

—DOLLY PARTON

NINE YEARS AFTER opening Dollywood, Dolly Parton debuted her most beloved accomplishment yet—one that happened to be her father's personal favorite. But rather than cut another chart-topping album or dream up another successful theme park, the country superstar set off on a whole new trail in 1995 by creating Dolly Parton's Imagination Library.

As part of her larger nonprofit organization, the Dollywood Foundation, Imagination Library sends young children one new age-appropriate book a month, for free, from birth through their fifth birthday, beginning with the cherished nursery classic *The Little Engine That Could*. And while the children's literacy

Be a Leader

program originally only impacted children from Sevier County, Tennessee, it has since expanded across all 50 states and beyond, donating more than one million books a month to mold young minds as far as Australia, the United Kingdom and the Republic of Ireland.

But true to Dolly's nature, the inspiration behind this wildly generous endeavor was sparked by the memories of her youth and her love for her father, Robert "Lee" Parton, a hardscrabble farmer who, though remarkably intelligent, had never learned to read or write. As Dolly told National Public Radio in 2018, "If you can read, even if you can't afford education, you can go on and learn about anything you want to know…it's important for kids to be encouraged to read, to dream and to plan for a better life and better future."

It's this selfless, no-strings-attached act of love that impacts thousands of lives every day, a timeless reminder that each of us has the power to create a lasting legacy by serving others.

Dolly Parton performs
in Knoxville, Tennessee,
on May 28, 2014.

"We cannot direct the wind,
but we can adjust the sails."

DOLLY PARTON

There's No Time for Self-Pity

"Get down off the cross, honey, somebody needs the wood!"

—SHIRLEE KENYON, *STRAIGHT TALK* (1992)

AS CALL-IN therapist "Doctor Shirlee" Kenyon in *Straight Talk* (1992), Dolly plays a character whose work revolves around offering others her best words of wisdom. It's a position Shirlee loves dearly, and if her rapidly growing fan base is any indication, she's definitely the best woman for the job. But when one caller rambles on and on (and on) about feeling sorry for herself, Shirlee doesn't sugarcoat the truth: life isn't always fair.

"Why, even the Declaration of Independence only guarantees life, liberty and the pursuit of happiness," she says. "It doesn't say anything about fair. Doesn't even say you have the right to be happy. Just to pursue it."

Don't waste your precious time on self-pity. Pick yourself up and keep going. You'll feel better before you know it.

Dolly Parton in 1992.

Laughter is Good for the Soul

Every life, especially one well-lived, sees its share of joy and sorrow. In our worst moments of despair, laughter is a cathartic release, a promise that the grief we share will not last forever.

IN THE HEARTFELT classic *Steel Magnolias* (1989), Dolly's character, Truvy Jones, is devastated when her good friend M'Lynn Eatenton (Sally Field) loses her daughter to complications from Type 1 diabetes. Truvy and the rest of the southern belles—Louisa "Ouiser" Boudreaux (Shirley MacLaine), Clairee Belcher (Olympia Dukakis) and Annelle Dupuy-Desoto

Julia Roberts, Sally Field, Shirley MacLaine, Dolly Parton and Daryl Hannah in a publicity photo for *Steel Magnolias* (1989).

Laughter is Good for the Soul

(Daryl Hannah)—rally around their friend in her time of bereavement. Immediately after the funeral, a despondent M'Lynn bursts into tears over her daughter's untimely death, crying and shouting about how much she'd love to hit someone. Suddenly, the typically cheerful Clairee grabs an unsuspecting Ouiser, daring M'Lynn to take her best shot at the group's outspoken cynic. Stunned at Clairee's over-the-top antics, the group breaks out into laughter. Embarrassed by her outburst, M'Lynn later apologizes to Truvy, but the empathetic hairdresser pays no mind. If anything, she was glad to see her friend smile again, even briefly, on such a heartbreaking occasion, telling M'Lynn, "Laughter through tears is my favorite emotion."

Like her *Steel Magnolias*' counterpart, Dolly knows you take the sunshine with the rain, and that a genuine laugh can be just as healing as a good cry. You may one day find yourself in a similar situation, but the lesson remains the same: Even when things are at their most bleak, if you can find a reason to laugh, take comfort. You'll make it through.

Dolly Parton and Olympia Dukakis in a scene from *Steel Magnolias* (1989).

Les Paul, Dolly Parton, Chet Atkins and Freddie Fender gather backstage at the Grammy Awards, February 19, 1977. As of 2020, Dolly has earned 11 Grammy Awards.

The Sun Will Rise Tomorrow

"It's been a long dark night
And I've been a-waitin' for the morning
It's been a long hard fight
But I see a brand new day a-dawning"

—DOLLY PARTON, "LIGHT OF A CLEAR BLUE MORNING"

IKE ANYONE ELSE, Dolly has seen her share of heartbreak and she's not afraid to talk about it, especially if it helps others who might be struggling. In a 2019 interview on the podcast *Dolly Parton's America*, the self-proclaimed "backwoods Barbie" opened up about how a series of prolonged personal problems in the early 1980s began taking a toll on her

Dolly Parton at the Palm Restaurant in Las Vegas, Nevada, February 1, 1977.

The Sun Will Rise Tomorrow

mental and physical health. She fell into a deep depression, "broken down" in this newfound spiritual darkness, and began having "serious conversations with God" about what had been weighing so heavily on her heart.

At her lowest moment, Dolly suddenly heard her dog, Popeye, coming down the hall. He hopped onto her bed, snapping her out of her desperate thoughts in the blink of an eye. "God is dog spelled backwards," she says of that time, "and I always thought that might have been the very thing." Rather than succumb to hopelessness and despair, she got the help she needed and kept moving forward.

Her 1977 song, "Light of a Clear Blue Morning," is a joyful message of hope. The clouds have parted, the darkness has lifted and there's a brand new day ahead—another chance to live life to its fullest. Decades of stardom and financial success have not made Dolly immune to the pain of weathering life's storms; she just keeps holding out for the rainbows.

The darkness doesn't last. You don't have to see the light to know it's coming your way.

Dolly Parton
in 1977.

"*Dreams are of no value if they're not equipped with wings!*"

⁓

DOLLY PARTON

Love is the Spice of Life

"Love is like a butterfly, a rare and gentle thing"

—DOLLY PARTON, "LOVE IS LIKE A BUTTERFLY"

LONG KNOWN AS her signature song, "Love Is Like a Butterfly" features the emblem of Dolly's colorful, spirited approach to life. As she once told *USA Today*, "Butterflies are my symbol. As a child, I used to get lost chasing them and got my butt whipped for wandering too far off. So we have butterflies everywhere." The "W" in the iconic sign of her beloved theme park, Dollywood, is arguably her most memorable butterfly to date.

Dolly performs in front of City Hall in New York City on August 21, 1978.

Love is the Spice of Life

With fluttering piano and breezy vocals, the warm and gentle hit track made for Dolly's consecutive third No. 1 single on the *Billboard* country charts.

Released in 1974, the same year she ended her professional relationship with Porter Wagoner to strike out on her own, "Love Is Like a Butterfly" reveals a mature singer ready to emerge from her cocoon, primed to leave her mentor's shadow for good. As a spiritual successor to "I Will Always Love You," the hit ballad she crafted to announce her parting with Wagoner, the song centers on the driving force in Dolly's life: love. In this case, romance takes center stage, with Dolly blissfully ruminating on the joys that come not merely from amorous advances but raw honesty, the brave beauty of letting others see us as we are.

The transformative freedom to create and live authentically speaks to the whole of Dolly Parton's presence. Free to be herself, she continues to captivate and inspire audiences of all walks of life.

There's no greater joy than allowing yourself to be loved for who you are.

Dolly Parton spreads her wings onstage in a Bob Mackie "butterfly" dress in the 1970s.

Take Pride in Your Work

"Tumble outta bed and I stumble to the kitchen
Pour myself a cup of ambition"

—DOLLY PARTON, "9 TO 5"

THERE'S NO QUESTION that to succeed in life takes hard work, a thick skin and a great deal of gumption. As Dolly knows, there's no becoming a musical legend overnight—you've got to put in your dues and chase your dreams with laser focus. With a little luck, you'll find a way to pay the bills doing something that makes the most of your skills and talents, something you love. But no matter how you put money in the

Dolly Parton as
Doralee Rhodes
in *9 to 5* (1980).

Take Pride in Your Work

bank, one thing's for sure: You've got to take pride in your work.

Written specifically for her film debut, *9 to 5* (1980), the titular song celebrates the tenacity in everyone who leans in and puts their nose to the grindstone week after week. But there's another layer to this worker's anthem—a shoutout to all the women in the workforce who keep soldiering on, even when the deck is stacked against them.

Turned down for the big promotion, only to see it go to a less-experienced coworker? Watched someone else take credit for your ideas? Ever been on the business-end of your boss's hair trigger temper? Dolly's here to cheer you on, pouring out sympathy like you dream of pouring one out with friends come Friday night. "You're just a step on the boss-man's ladder," she sings knowingly. "But you got dreams he'll never take away," dreams that will get you through this work week and beyond.

No matter how you make a living, do the best job you can right where you are. At the end of the day, it's your name on that paycheck and nobody else's.

Dolly Parton, Lily Tomlin and Jane Fonda attend the New York City première of *9 to 5* in 1980.

Linda Ronstadt, Dolly Parton and Emmylou Harris enjoy the sunshine at Dolly's home in Brentwood, Tennessee, in 1978.

"Don't get so busy
making a living that you forget
how to make a life."

DOLLY PARTON

Dolly Parton
c. 1985.

Honor Your Roots

Give thanks for your blessings, triumphs and
other successes by looking out for those less fortunate,
especially when you know their struggles firsthand. Chances are,
you wouldn't be where you are today without them.

NO MATTER WHERE her travels might take her,
Dolly always speaks fondly of her home state of
Tennessee. After racking up platinum albums like
Here You Come Again and *Once Upon a Christmas*, the platinum
blonde decided to give back to the community that made her in a
bold new way.

During a 1983 interview with Terry Wogan, Dolly confided, "I
have an idea that I've had for years that's beginning to become a
reality." She was speaking, of course, about opening her own theme
park in Tennessee, a sort of Smoky Mountain Disneyland that
would showcase the uniquely Southern way of living that shaped
her identity. Luckily, she didn't have to look far for inspiration: Just

Honor Your Roots

10 miles from her childhood home sat Silver Dollar City, a humble backwoods amusement park that presented Dolly with a lucrative new opportunity. The savvy businesswoman knew a deal when she saw one; she joined forces with Silver Dollar City in a deal to "Dolly-ize" the humble mountain retreat, and on May 3, 1986, the gates to "the friendliest town in the Smokies" swung open under a brand new name: Dollywood.

Within its first year of operation, attendance at Dollywood skyrocketed from 750,000 to more than 1.3 million smiling guests and is a large reason why Pigeon Forge, Tennessee, is such a thriving family vacation destination. But beyond its thrilling rides, colorful live shows and other family-friendly amusements, today, this country-themed tourist attraction provides 4,000 Tennesseans with stable jobs and opportunities for sustained economic growth—in other words, a long term means to escape the poverty Dolly once knew as a child. And while few of us can afford to open our own theme park, we can certainly remember that success is best shared by paying it forward however we can.

Dolly Parton and Reba McEntire celebrate the 60th anniversary of the Grand Ole Opry in 1986.

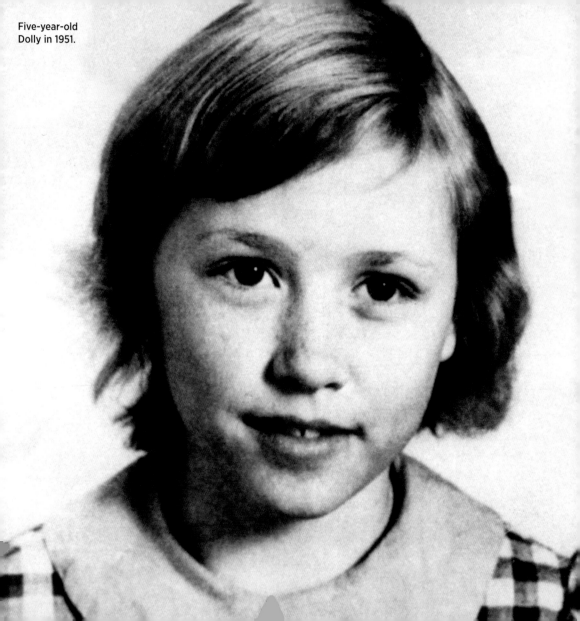

Five-year-old
Dolly in 1951.

Happiness Is a Choice

"No amount of money could buy from me
The memories that I have of then
No amount of money could pay me
To go back and live through it again"

—DOLLY PARTON, "IN THE GOOD OLD DAYS (WHEN TIMES WERE BAD)"

HAVING GROWN UP in dire straits, no one would have blamed a young Dolly Parton if she had sought to distance herself from her Smoky Mountain roots after making it on the country music scene. But rather than try to forget those difficult times by basking in the creature comforts of fame and wealth, Dolly has long looked to her childhood in Sevierville as a

Happiness Is a Choice

source of inspiration—a reservoir of precious memories from which she draws not only new material but endless strength. There's no better evidence of this than her 1969 track "In the Good Old Days (When Times Were Bad)," a song in which she lays bare the images of her youth she'll never forget.

"I've seen daddy's hands break open and bleed," she sings, "And I've seen him work 'til he's stiff as a board / An' I've seen momma lay and suffer in sickness / In need of a doctor we couldn't afford."

And yet, despite the abject misery of her upbringing, Dolly insists she wouldn't trade a single experience for all the money in the world.

The Partons may have lacked what most of us would call bare necessities, but it's clear their ramshackle cabin was filled to the rafters with love, and that she considers her childhood a happy one. "I don't have any sympathy for myself," she says, " 'cause it took all that to make all this. . . . Some people work at being miserable. I work at being happy." Every day, we can follow Dolly's lead by choosing to make the best of whatever life offers us.

Dolly Parton
c. 1981.

"Leave something good in every day."

DOLLY PARTON

Dolly performs on the *Phil Donahue Show* on April 30, 1977. In 1976, the singer had her own variety show, *Dolly*, which ran for one season.

Media Lab Books
For inquiries, call 646-838-6637

Copyright 2020 Topix Media Lab

Published by Topix Media Lab
14 Wall Street, Suite 4B
New York, NY 10005

Printed in China

ISBN-13: 978-1-948174-61-9
ISBN-10: 1-948174-61-8

CEO Tony Romando

Vice President & Publisher Phil Sexton
Senior Vice President of Sales & New Markets Tom Mifsud
Vice President of Retail Sales & Logistics Linda Greenblatt
Director of Finance Vandana Patel
Manufacturing Director Nancy Puskuldjian
Financial Analyst Matthew Quinn
Brand Marketing & Promotions Assistant Emily McBride

Chief Content Officer Jeff Ashworth
Director of Editorial Operations Courtney Kerrigan
Creative Director Steven Charny
Photo Director Dave Weiss
Executive Editor Tim Baker

Content Editor Juliana Sharaf
Art Director Susan Dazzo
Senior Editor Trevor Courneen
Designer Kelsey Payne
Copy Editor & Fact Checker Tara Sherman

Co-Founders Bob Lee, Tony Romando

COVER: Michael Ochs Archives/Getty Images